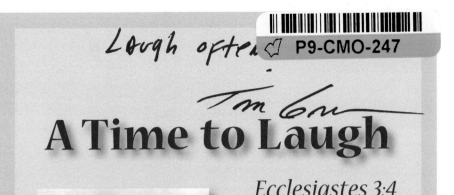

A Time to Laugh

Ecclesiastes 3:4

One man's witness that ministry is not all
Preaching, Praying, and Piosity

Tom Graves

Design and production by EverCom
Production assistance by Betty Taylor

Starfish Publishing Company PMB#728
5100 Eldorado Pkwy., Ste. 102
McKinney, TX 75070
www.StarfishPublishingCompany.com
903-784-8151

This book is dedicated to

Cleopatra

the cat who is queen of the
Red River and makes me
chuckle, laugh, guffaw, and roar
with her crazy feline antics.

Contents

Foreword

In my lifetime the church has dealt with some thorny and controversial issues. Sometimes we do it well, sometimes we stumble and blunder. Because we are worldwide and democratic, there are often bitter divisions on questions about which many are passionate: women in ministry, the empowerment of the laity, abortion, war, the ordination of openly gay candidates for ministry, the preservation of our planet's environment, to mention only a few.

These serious challenges have been and are being dealt with quite somberly. In the future there will be others to challenge our faith and our judgments.

The writer of Ecclesiastes reminds us that, "There is a time for everything," including a time to weep and a time to laugh (3:4). We affirm that Jesus was the Word made flesh and was fully human and fully divine. Since we know from John 11:35 that Jesus wept at the death of his friend Lazarus, we can be certain that he also laughed at the truly funny things in life.

This man, who proclaimed that God cared for us all, even the birds of the air and the lilies of the field, must have laughed a lot when his followers argued about the best places in the kingdom, didn't want to be bothered with children, and were scandalized when he ate with the rabble of his day.

In the midst of the serious issues of the church and the abounding, sacrificial love of Jesus, I am convinced that we do not laugh enough at the sublime and the ridiculous words and events that occur in our life together as disciples. With this in mind, this volume has emerged as I have remembered the truly funny things in my fifty-plus years as a United Methodist minister.

Most of these stories are firsthand accounts and some are tales told to me by others. Together they present a mosaic of human foibles and ridiculous occurrences which, in retrospect, make us chuckle, giggle, and sometimes openly guffaw!

I hope they will bring some fun into your reading and lighten your spirit for a while.

I am indebted to many for these accounts. The names have been changed to protect the author and help him avoid entering the witness protection program in self-defense!

I am especially grateful, as always, to Betty Taylor, my agent and coach for no pay, who sticks with me; and to Joan Lathen, our superb editor, to Dean Dickschat of EverCom, our talented designer, and to my good friend Mike House, for invaluable technical assistance.

My sincere thanks to Ralph Kozak for his gracious permission to reproduce "Jesus Laughing" on the cover.

Be faithful, live well, and laugh often!

Tom Graves

Chapter One

And a Little Child Shall Lead Them into Laughter

Children in church are a source of wonder and wisdom with an uninhibited way of disarming us all. Their freshness and spontaneity are priceless and offer a striking reminder of a way in which Jesus taught. Ira Williams, retired minister and author, puts it this way:

They were all sitting around talking man talk, and Jesus put a child in their midst.

The people were growing restless in their conduct and their conversation, and Jesus put a child in their midst.

The twelve were beginning to feel they had learned all they needed to know to be good disciples, and Jesus put a child in their midst.

His followers were getting anxious to reach the business community and the so-called right people, and Jesus put a child in their midst.

The twelve took a long look at their arrogance and their careless deeds and their need to learn the consequences of their actions and the worth of a human soul, because Jesus put a child in their midst.

Children have provided me with some rare moments, a few of which I share in this chapter, "And a Little Child Shall Lead Them into Laughter."

A Sunday School teacher was expounding on the story of Noah to his class of children. He asked of the lads, "Johnny, do you think Noah did a lot of fishing while he was on the ark?" "No," replied Johnny. "How could he with only two worms?"

A young girl, sitting beside Johnny, added, "He couldn't have been a very smart man because he took two termites with him on a wooden boat!"

Another Sunday School teacher was describing how Lot's wife looked back and turned into a pillar of salt. She expected some consternation from her young class, but Jess replied, "That's nothing. My mom looked back once and turned into a telephone pole!"

Then there was Charlie, who responded to the question "Who was Peter in the Bible?" with, "I fink he was a wabbit!"

During Advent the youth choir was rehearsing a carol to the tune of Brahm's Lullaby. After several run-throughs, Sarah's hand shot up and she asked, "Why don't we sing something more adultery?"

Jerry was a round-faced Charlie Brownish kind of child who never missed a Children's Time in worship. He rarely said anything, but listened intently to everything I said.

I usually met the children on the chancel steps early in the worship service, wearing my pulpit robe and stole. Jerry never took his eyes off of me and always waved good-bye as he headed off to Children's Church in another room.

One Wednesday morning he and the other children in our weekday program brought the office staff Halloween cupcakes iced in orange as a surprise. As the cupcakes were distributed and we thanked them appropriately, I could see Jerry's eyes fixed on me, in my street clothes, trying to figure out where he had seen me before. As the group exited, he was the last to leave. He paused at the door, turned back with an "aha" look on his open face, and exclaimed as he waved, "Bye, Jesus!"

My secretary, Alice, who knew me well, said, "I need to have a talk with that young man and set him straight."

My favorite Children's Time story is about Neal, a blue-eyed blond about four years old. He loved to talk, responded to every question I would ask, and always contributed something to Children's Time in worship. His mother was our Director of Education and a proud parent of this her only child.

One spring Sunday I brought a budding willow limb and showed the children that spring was in the air. "What is happening to this limb?" I asked. "It's growing!" was the enthusiastic response.

"How many of you are growing?" I ventured. Every little hand went up, waving in eager affirmation. I ventured further, "How many of you are learning?" Well, about half would acknowledge they were learning something, so I probed for the kinds of things learned.

"I learned to tie my shoes." "I learned to write cursive." "I learned to roller skate." And the list lengthened. Neal, on the top step of the chancel, was silent, his brow wrinkled to indicate a concentrated effort to think of something he was learning. Uncharacteristically, no words came.

The responses died down and I prepared to offer a prayer of thanks to God for learning, when Neal's hand shot up. "What are you learning, Neal?" I responded. Then, in his deep voice, at a volume level that everyone in the cavernous sanctuary could hear plainly, he said, "I learned to zip my pants!" I could see his mother sliding down in the pew as the congregation began to laugh. Not wanting Neal to feel ridiculed, I tried to recover with the inane response, "Well, that's a really important thing to know how to do." The choir collapsed in laughter at me, and all was well.

I seriously doubt that Neal, now a wonderfully productive adult, remembers that Sunday at all. I do.

Ruth Ann was in my confirmation class one spring. Her mother was our volunteer choir director at Saint Andrew's and the president of United Methodist Women. She ate, slept, and breathed missional ministries. If you visited her house, you might have to move unfolded laundry for her family of five to find a place to sit, but she would have every UMW related piece of mission material at her fingertips. She was indeed a wonder.

On the first day of class, I asked the children in confirmation to tell me about themselves, where they were born, their families and friends. When it became Ruth Ann's turn, she began with, "I was born at Methodist Hospital, but my mother couldn't be there. She was at a circle meeting."

Some stories require background information and this is one of them.

My very first sermon as anyone's pastor was preached at Grove Hill, the smallest numerical and one of the largest spirited congregations I served in fifty-plus years. The Keene family was a whole new experience for me. Roy Lee, the dad, was a free-lance carpenter. Edna Mae was the mom and bore him thirteen children, seven boys and six girls. They were quite a clan.

They lived in a simple house on a hillside sloping down from the road. Every time a new child arrived, Roy simply built another room on the house. It was rambling, interesting, and hard to describe.

As new ones came along, the older children became junior parents, each having their own younger charge to tend and nurture. It was a system that worked very well for them and was a wonder to me, an only child. Eating a meal at their long rectangular picnic table built by Roy Lee was a major culinary adventure. They invited me often and there was always plenty to eat. It was simple but good.

Roy Lee and Edna Mae rarely came to church, but they wanted their children there and saw that they were all cleaned and scrubbed on Sunday morning. When their pickup arrived, with Alvin Lee, the "John Boy" of the family, driving, and children all over the vehicle, our Sunday School attendance doubled automatically.

Several of the younger children had pronounced speech impediments of various kinds and called me "Budder Tom," their version of "Brother Tom." The six-year-old son, Bobby Lee, went to visit his grandparents for a week one summer, and they sent him to Vacation Bible School at their church, an ultraconservative pietistic congregation. He heard a lot about sin, backsliding, repentance, and God's judgment that week and returned home on Saturday.

Sunday night services were fairly informal at Grove Hill, with a lot of singing and a prayer time at the chancel. I invited anyone who wanted to pray there to come, and I was available to pray with those who asked for it.

To my surprise, Bobby Lee was the first one to kneel and immediately raised his hand for me to join him. I did. He looked at me tearfully and said, "Budder Tom, I backfired," and confessed that he had teased his younger sister and was very sorry for his behavior. Inside I was laughing, but my face had a fatherly/pastoral smile as I told him that a lot of brothers fall into that habit and I was sure God understood and forgave his young soul. He promised not to do it again, and as he arose to go back to his seat, he hugged my neck and kissed me. I knew the motor of his heart was now clear of the soot of the "backfire" and humming right along in his six-year-old body.

Ah, that all of us were as sensitive to the moral "backfires" of our lives. Peace might be more than a distant dream. Jesus had it right. "A little child shall lead them."

Chapter Two

An Angel Factory It's Not

Preparing for the ministry as a student in college and seminary is a challenging and fascinating time which is only understood from inside the experience.

In seminary, we were referred to by the undergraduates on the hill as "The Angel Factory," or "The God Squad." On reflection I can assure you that we were neither. We were simply human beings who had heard a clarion call to be something we had never been before, and in the stress of preparing for that, some hilarious events occurred. This chapter recounts some of those.

A classmate of mine had spent the summer selling Bibles in Appalachia for the Southwest Publishing Company. He went from house to house, making his pitch to mountain people, whose way of life was totally strange to this young man from Plainview, Texas.

One particularly hot and humid July day, he approached a hillside cabin and knocked on the door. He was sweaty and panting from the climb. A woman answered the door. Her hair was tied with a bandana and her face reflected the hard life she had lived. He noticed wet snuff dripping down her chin as she offered her gnarled hand to greet him.

"Ma'am," he began, "I'd like to show you this wonderful Bible for your family. It's the newest translation, the Revised Standard Version." She stiffened and replied, "Oh, no, we don't read nothin' but the Saint John's Virgin in this house."

Not wanting to offend the young man, the woman

offered him a drink of cold water before he went on his way. He accepted gladly and then she proceeded to lead him across the yard to the well. When she raised the bucket, brimming with clear water, she took a dipper and handed it to him for a sample. He again noticed the snuff-stained lips and chin and, in an instant, decided the only way to handle the situation was to drink from the dipper right next to the handle, thereby avoiding swallowing snuff-flavored well water.

Just as he swallowed the first dipper full, she exclaimed, "Well, I swear, you're the only person I've seen who drinks out of a dipper just like I do."

He swallowed hard, nodded his gratitude, and fled down the mountain!

Homiletics is the art of preaching, and in homiletics class every student preaches a few times each year and is evaluated by the professor and the class members.

Jack had never preached, even in his home church or to his youth group, so, unlike most of us, he was clueless and terrified of the experience. We were called on alphabetically and he could see his time was coming soon.

He studied, he fretted, he worried, he wrote and rewrote. When the time finally came, he slinked to the lectern, read the entire sermon from his manuscript in monotone, and never looked up from the page. It was sad.

After he sat down, the class sat silently, holding our collective breath and waiting for the first comment from our professor, known for his tough critiques.

Finally, he spoke: "Jack," he said, "your preaching's not bad." We let out a collective sigh of relief, and so did Jack. Then he continued, "It's tragic!"

Jack did a meltdown. We loved and worked with him all semester with the wise support of the professor, and he became a very promising preacher who is still ministering effectively in an urban setting.

Since then, I've had a few sermons of my own that were not only bad but tragic. Thankfully, that does not limit what God can do with them.

One of my classmates was the student pastor of three small rural churches, and somehow he felt he was God's gift to evangelism. He was very proud of never using a note or a manuscript when he preached. When others of us would challenge the wisdom of that, his response would be, "God will tell me what to say and I will say it."

One Sunday he based his sermon on the Matthew 5:28 text, which admonishes the hearers that "looking lustfully on a woman is committing adultery in the heart." He waxed eloquently and emotionally about purity of heart and the dangers of evil thinking. As he approached the climax of the sermon, his voice became more intense and his gestures more exaggerated as he headed toward the clincher.

"You can commit robbery with your heart as well as you can with your hands," he began. "You can commit murder with your heart as well as you can with your gun," he continued. "And, you can commit adultery with your heart as well as you can with your, with your, with your … well you can!"

That story got back to campus before he did!

I think after that he began to take a few notes to the pulpit with him.

This same classmate was so full of himself that, on a snowy winter morning, he refused to cancel the service. When he arrived at the church designated for worship that Sunday, one lone farmer was there with a fire going in the potbellied stove.

Undaunted, he preached his sermon to the lone layman.

When he asked for a response, the farmer drawled, "Well, preacher, it was okay, but when I pull my truck full of hay into a pasture and only one old cow shows up, I don't give her the whole load."

One fellow student, who had spent his life in the city, was appointed to a rural parish where most of his parishioners were farmers. He knew nothing about farming but sincerely wanted to be accepted and become "one of the folks."

On his first day, he went out to visit one of his members who was in the field on a tractor. "Brother Johnson," the pastor began. "What a fine looking farm you have here. You and God have done a great job with this land." The farmer responded, "Yeah, but you should have seen it when God had it all by himself!"

Looking around, the pastor noticed the farmer's son, just returned from a year in college. He was plowing behind a mule-drawn steel plow. "That's my son, Zeke," the farmer boasted. "He used to get to the end of that turn row and say, 'Whoa, Beck, gee, get on around there.' But now," the farmer beamed, "Zeke's got learnin'. He gets to the end of that cotton row and he says, 'Halt, Rebecca, pivot and proceed.'"

On Sunday night, the young pastor, wanting to be folksy and informal, came to the end of the service, looked into the congregation, and spotted farmer Johnson in the back row. "Brother Johnson," he called, "would you say the closing prayer tonight?" There was a long silence, broken by Brother Johnson's voice saying, "Pray yourself. That's what we pay you for!"

On another occasion, the same student pastor preached an impassioned plea for repentance and conversion and gave an emotional invitation for the congregation to come to the chancel and kneel and pray and begin again. But no one came.

Frustrated, he then asked for those who would simply like to make a new dedication of themselves to come. No response.

In desperation he asked for those who wanted to be prayed for to raise their hands. No one did.

Finally, he challenged, "Will everyone who wants to go to heaven stand up?" Everyone stood but Brother Johnson. The pastor responded, "Brother Johnson, don't you want to go to heaven when you die?" "Oh, yeah," was the response. "I do when I die, but I thought you were gettin' up a load for tonight!"

At my first student pastorate, we had a summer revival in August. Having some promotional blood in me, I decided to make each night special with a theme: "Bring your Bible night," "Bring your neighbor night," "favorite hymn night," and so on.

It was harvesttime, and so I designated one night as "Come as you are night." I announced it early in the week by saying, "Now Thursday night is 'Come as you are night.' Just leave the fields and come as you are to church."

After the first service, a woman approached me, saying, "Brother Graves, we're hot and sweating and smelly at the end of the day, so maybe you should say that in a different way." Realizing she had a point, I revised my announcement and said, "Now, Thursday night is 'Come as you are night.' Just leave the fields, take a bath, and come as you are."

We had a big crowd that night as I recall.

Our volunteer choir director was a stunning beauty with a spectacular figure which was accented by her tight-fitting clothes. Her name, appropriately enough, was Celestial. We had an abundance of men in the choir admiring the celestial body!

I added spice to the situation on Sunday with a misprint in the order of worship. I typed and printed the bulletin on a mimeograph machine, and one of the hymn titles read, "He Keeps Me Sinning."

On that same Sunday, our communion steward, who lived next door to the church, had been out of town and had forgotten it was communion Sunday. Realizing her omission, she rushed home and prepared the elements just in time for me to serve them to the congregation.

In her haste, she mistook the bottle of green

persimmon wine for grape juice, and so at the end of the service, we were all appropriately puckered and could have stood and whistled the Doxology!

One Mother's Day I was preaching what I thought was a truly fine and moving sermon about motherhood. It was a hot May day, and we had opened the windows of the sanctuary to let the breeze in, since there was no air conditioning in those days.

There was a large arrangement of roses in front of the pulpit, and through one of the open windows came a hummingbird. It would ascend to the peak of the ceiling, dive to the roses for a few moments, and then relocate. The only time the congregation looked my way was when the hummingbird hovered at the pulpit.

A very large woman with an oversized corsage was sitting on the back pew taking it all in. As the hummingbird hovered above us, I sensed impending doom. Sure enough, he spotted her corsage and went into a steep and speedy dive toward her chest. She let out a loud shriek and ran, all 280 pounds of her, for the back door.

So much for preaching that fine sermon. I said the benediction and went home.

A friend of mine was preaching at his rural church one Sunday night. There was no running water in that building, so he always kept a bottle of water in the trunk of his car in case he needed to baptize someone.

On this night, to his surprise, a young man came forward to take the vows of baptism and church membership. The pastor sent one of the laymen to get the water from the trunk of his car, and to fill the font with water from the carefully stowed bottle.

In his haste in the darkness of the parking area, the man grabbed the wrong bottle for the filling, and my friend ended up baptizing his young convert with 7-Up!

"I thought it felt a little sticky," he said later.

I'm sure God didn't care.

I could go on, but you get the picture that a large part of theological education takes place outside the classroom and textbooks. It takes place with people who, to their credit, helped us learn and grow as we moved toward larger responsibilities.

They didn't call us students for nothing.

But angels we weren't!

Theological education is intense and mentally demanding. Sometimes the pressure mounts and those of us in the dorm have to do something to relieve the tension.

Here are a few examples:

Some roommates down the hall gave a party and

invited the whole floor. My roommate, Jim, and I went. Among the goodies offered was a large bowl of chocolate M & Ms. They got gobbled up in a hurry.

What we didn't know was that sprinkled in with the candy were some identical pieces which were medicinal and designed to turn the urine red for lab purposes. One of the party-givers got them from his dad, who was a pharmacist.

The next day I was standing next to Jim at the urinals and both our urine was bright red. Alarmed, he called his dad, a doctor, who told him it was a medicinal dye and not blood, so not to worry.

Revenge is sweet, so Jim went away for the weekend and I told the party hosts that he had a long-standing urinary infection and was so alarmed by the blood in his urine that he had flown home to Florida for a complete examination at the hospital.

They were horrified at the result of their prank. When Jim returned on Monday, they apologized abjectly, offering to pay for his round-trip flight to Miami, to do his laundry for the rest of the year, and to shine his shoes, and groveled before him in apologetic remorse.

He thanked them and waited two days to let them off the hook.

I think that was their last prank in the dorm.

One day when our dorm supervisor was away, we filled his room completely with wadded newspapers from floor to ceiling so that on his return, when he opened the door, there was only paper.

Once he cleaned his way inside, he also discovered all the furniture had been distributed to other rooms, and the scavenger hunt was on.

We never confessed to that one.

Then there was the time when the wedding of a very prominent family's daughter was scheduled for the seminary chapel. It was in all the papers as a North Dallas social event of the year, replete with orchestra, limousines, and an elaborate dinner reception at the Dallas Athletic Country Club.

It was snob heaven and we just couldn't resist.

We wheedled a tower key from the custodial staff, climbed up after the rehearsal in the dark of night, and changed out all the clear candlelike bulbs in the tower. We replaced them with red 100-watt dandies!

Only years after graduation, when our degrees were safe, did we tell anyone we did it.

But, it lived up to its press. It was a wedding to remember!

As I said earlier, angels we weren't. Imps, maybe, but not angels.

Chapter Three

Wrong Turns
in Church Rites

Rites and sacraments of the church are special occasions, and, as a result, considerable planning, intense interest, and high expectations are brought to the actual event. Baptisms, confirmations, weddings, funerals, consecrations, and ordinations are ripe for humor, because the slightest slipup is noticed by all.

Here are just a few examples:

During a children's sermon, I pointed to the baptismal font, always visible in the chancel, and asked the children if anyone knew what it was. One little girl's hand went up and I responded, "Susan, what is it?" With great confidence she replied, "It's a bird bath!"

In that same church, we did an extensive restoration on the one-hundred-year-old sanctuary over a period of six months. One of the stipulations we made with the contractor was the removal of all furniture not bolted down and the careful covering of all the rest during the painting and staining phase.

One Monday morning I walked into the chancel to see four big strong men wrestling with the marble baptismal font in an effort to move it out of harm's way. Their faces were red as they panted and sweated in the struggle. The font would not yield.

I approached them and said, "That font is anchored to the stone outcropping underneath this building. It has never been moved and I'm sure it never will be, unless an earthquake strikes Navarro County."

Amazed, and relieved, the men gave up the effort,

threw a covering over the font, and said, "Thanks, pastor. You saved us from a quartet of hernias!"

It is nice to know that some things just don't move.

United Methodist churches do not have baptistries but offer immersion if the candidate feels strongly about that mode of baptism. On one occasion, a man requested immersion because of his family's Baptist background, so the pastor borrowed the baptistry at the Disciples of Christ Church nearby.

The waders provided for the guest pastor were very large to accommodate the size and weight of the pastor of that church, but he dutifully put them on, waded into the water, and signaled the candidate to follow him into the pool. With family and friends watching, he held his convert and bent over for the immersion. When he did, the boots immediately filled with water and the weight of that much liquid dragged the pastor into the water with the young baptismal candidate. Dripping wet, he stood up, poured water on the candidate's head, blubbered the vows, and closed with a prayer.

Makes you wonder what kind of waders John the Baptist might have worn in the Jordan River.

A priest and his rabbi friend/rival lived next door to each other in an upscale suburb, both pastors of churches with considerable means.

The rabbi noticed that the priest was having his entire lawn relandscaped by professionals, so he proceeded to do the same at his house and go one better by adding a large fountain in the middle of the circular drive.

The priest then showed up one day driving a brand-new Mercedes Benz, parked in plain view in his front drive. Not to be outdone, the rabbi came home the next day in a shiny new Jaguar.

Feeling satisfied and a little smug, he looked out at his new vehicle the next morning and, lo and behold, the priest was sprinkling holy water on his Mercedes.

After pondering the significance of this sacramental show, the rabbi marched out to his driveway with a hacksaw and cut off two inches of the tailpipe!

Ah, the joy of the ecumenical spirit.

Weddings are, without a doubt, the most intense and challenging of the ceremonies of the church. So much attention from so many people, large amounts of money, and an unrealistic desire for perfection make a perfect combination for disaster.

I've seen a few.

I was presiding at a wedding in which the floor furnace grate was directly centered in front of the chancel rail. It was a hot summer day long before church buildings were air conditioned with anything more than ceiling fans. All the men were perspiring in their tuxedos, and I was almost soaked beneath the clerical black robe I was wearing.

After the blessing of the rings, I offered the bride's

ring to the groom to be placed on the bride's finger while he said the appropriate vow. He was nervous and his hands were damp. The ring slipped from between his fingers and "kerplunk" was the sickening sound it made as it landed in the duct beneath the grate.

I borrowed a ring from a bridesmaid and we proceeded with the vows. After the ceremony, some of the groomsmen took a long broom handle, covered the end with sticky chewing gum, and, with the aid of a flashlight, retrieved the vanished ring and returned it to the groom in the receiving line. With newly dried hands, he took it and placed it on his bride's finger.

"With this ring I thee wed and then with this ring I thee wed."

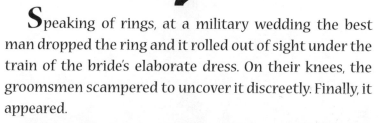

Speaking of rings, at a military wedding the best man dropped the ring and it rolled out of sight under the train of the bride's elaborate dress. On their knees, the groomsmen scampered to uncover it discreetly. Finally, it appeared.

Not wanting to appear flustered, I changed the liturgy to "Here is the ring. Pick it up, and place it on her finger, repeating after me ..."

And then there was the one in which the groom discovered, after arriving at the church, that he had left the ring box on the roof of his car in the haste to get everything else loaded. We proceeded with the ceremony and sent a friend back to the groom's house, hoping he could find it. Remarkably he did find it in the gutter of the street and brought it to the reception to replace the cigar band we had used as a substitute.

I was asked to assist in the wedding for the son of good friends. His fiancée was a member of a very formal high church and the ceremony was to be held there.

At the rehearsal the most reverend and the very reverend priests didn't quite know what to do with me, since the rules of their church prohibited any minister not in their communion from doing anything in the altar area. So, they finally decided that I could deliver a greeting and read a brief lesson. Robed and wearing a stole, that's what I did and then sat to view the elaborate ceremony, complete with bells and incense.

At the reception dinner table, my son-in-law said, "Tom, now we finally know just what you are. You are the slightly reverend!"

Oh well, better to be slightly reverend than irreverent!

And then there was my own wedding.

Linda and I married at her home church, First United Methodist of Paris, Texas. It was packed with family, friends, neighbors, and members of my three rural churches.

It was a hot September night, and the wax candles were beginning to yield to the heat, slowly bending downward. As we knelt at the chancel for the prayers, I noticed out of the corner of my eye that one of the tapers was falling to the canvas under the candelabra. I felt sure it would go out on the way down, but it didn't and it set the canvas on fire.

The custodian rushed out and extinguished the flame with a wet towel. When we arose for the benediction, a cloud of white smoke was ascending to the dome of the sanctuary.

Some of my so-called friends remarked that they weren't sure whether they had been at a wedding or the election of a new pope!

On an unusually warm July night, the best man had too much to drink at a prewedding party and threw up on the bride at the "til death us do part" moment in the covenant.

The four-year-old ring bearer forgot his father's admonition to stop by the "little boys' room" before the processional and urinated on the leg of a groomsman during the vows. The bride fainted and medical attention ensued on the altar floor while the congregation squirmed in discomfort.

At my very first wedding as pastor of a large suburban church, the father of the bride, who objected to the marriage, which was interracial, arrived drunk. He was a prominent member of the church and the community.

The father was arrested and escorted from the church by the local police before the ceremony, which proceeded with a police officer at every door and the back of every aisle. Tensions were sky high, to say the least.

When I arrived home later that evening, Linda was ironing my shirt for the next morning. "How'd it go?" she asked cheerfully.

"Don't ask."

My worst was what has become known as "The Wedding from Hell." This is the unabridged version of that fateful Saturday night.

One of my daughter's friends was to be married in June. The church to which her family belonged was too small to seat all the friends and family, and so she asked if she could be married in our sanctuary and if I would perform the ceremony. I agreed.

As Murphy's Law would have it, our fine organist got the flu and a substitute was brought in at the last minute. She was nice enough but had never touched a large pipe organ before. She practiced diligently for a couple of afternoons and sounded acceptable, but not good.

Among the guests at the wedding was a very large, tall woman with a beehive hairdo. The color was blonde from a bottle and her clothes were flamboyant. Pink flowing dress, yellow shoes and bag, and a lot of jewelry. With her was her three-year-old son. They were seated near the rear of the sanctuary, in a pew which was elevated several steps above the aisle. The boy was restless but not a disturbance.

I had arranged with the organist to watch for my

signal, a nod after the recessional, lower the volume, and allow me to make the announcement to the congregation about the reception.

All went well, and when the time came, I nodded. The organ was at full volume for the recessional, and she couldn't manage to make it softer. I nodded again to no avail, and then it happened. The woman in the pink dress decided this was a good time to make a quick exit.

With the little boy in tow, she moved toward the aisle in a hurry. Disaster was imminent and there was nothing I could do. Sure enough, she forgot the steps, plunged spread-eagle to the aisle, shaking the building with the impact, and began to scream, "O Lordy! O Lordy!" Meanwhile, the three-year-old was jumping up and down in the aisle, yelling, "I want big Daddy! I want big Daddy!" I was still nodding at the organist, but nothing changed.

At this point the bride's muscular brother, in a suit two sizes too small, spied the woman in the aisle. Beached whale comes to mind! He was the head usher, and his thought seemed not to be "Is she hurt?" but "We gotta clear that aisle." Fantasizing that he could get his hands under her arms and leverage her up, he charged. The ensuing scene was that of a large wheelbarrow going rapidly backward as the woman dug her high heels into the carpet and pushed the butch brother into the back wall of the church. She then stood upright and grabbed the boy and they exited to the tune of "I want big Daddy!"

With a gesture, I dismissed the congregation to deafening organ music and headed to the house.

When I arrived, my irreverent children were re-enacting the entire lovely scene, complete with my son, Mark, mimicking all my expressions of dismay and disgust.

I just don't get no respect.

I could go on, but you get the picture. After more than a thousand weddings, there are bound to be a few strange ones.

Maybe that's why "For better or for worse" is still included in the vows. Sometimes worse comes sooner than later.

Ah, funerals. They can be tough, but in general they are easier than weddings.

Once in Georgetown, one of our laymen bought an old used hearse for his high-school-aged daughter to drive to school. It was considered "so cool" by her friends.

Our custodian, Pedro Gonzalez, arrived one Monday morning and spied the hearse parked by the church, which was across University Avenue from the high school. Frantically, he began to dust and pick up and vacuum the vast sanctuary, which was not his usual Monday agenda.

I walked in and asked why the hurry. With wild gestures he pointed to the Ash Street doors, saying, "Bury! Bury! Bury!"

After several minutes of convincing, he began to realize that this was the funeral that never was.

A young green pastor in his first assignment was warned by the funeral director on the way to an East Texas cemetery that the ground was sandy and would often cave in with weight, so he should not stand close to the grave while doing the committal. Confident that he knew better than his hick funeral director, the pastor stepped right to the grave to begin, and as the grave walls crumbled, he fell completely into the grave.

Stunned, the grieving family and friends could hear him rattling around in the casket-lowering apparatus at the bottom of the grave. In a few moments, his head appeared through the velvet curtains around the base of the casket.

The silence was awkward until the son of the deceased began to laugh. Everyone joined in the humor and helped the poor pastor out of the grave. He stepped back and then back some more before beginning with "Dearly beloved…"

And then there was the arrival at a cemetery grave site, only to discover that it was the wrong grave. The dispatcher had sent identical hearses with bad instructions.

So here we were, trading grave sites with another funeral party, and waving as we passed them on the lane.

It was my only experience at playing "Musical Hearses."

And then there was the one for the hippie who had gotten stoned on LSD, lain down on the railroad track, and been killed by the engine of a speeding train. His friends had no church and came to me to give him a decent burial. The undertaker and I decided we should do the humane thing, and so we did.

It all went fairly well until the final blessing, after which his buddies took off all their clothes, grabbed their guitars, played and danced on the grave, while their girlfriends circled around and sang.

I am glad now that this was long before video cameras!

My first funeral was in November of my initial year as pastor. Hank, the town reprobate, died suddenly. For years he had failed to hold a steady job, pay his bills, relate to his family and former friends, be a contributing member of society, or stay sober. He eked by on a meager pension and the begrudging alms of a decreasing number of neighbors who felt sorry for him. Through it all he maintained a kind of aloof arrogance that isolated him from everyone. On the day of his death, his son called from out of town to ask if I would conduct his funeral in our church and arrange for six pallbearers. Believing everyone, even Hank, deserved a decent burial, I agreed. It would be my first.

No one wanted to be Hank's pallbearer. He had lied and cheated his way into so many bad relationships that I couldn't find anyone who was mildly willing. By using the "It's our Christian duty" ploy, I finally managed to convince six of my faithful laymen to close their businesses for an afternoon, put on ties and suits, and carry Hank's casket to the grave.

Befitting Hank's personality, it was a bitterly cold and rainy afternoon. His small family and a few dutiful members of the church attended the service, in which I read a lot of Scripture and talked a lot about God, not being able to say a whole lot about Hank.

I rode in the hearse with the funeral director ahead of the pallbearers' limo, grateful at that point that we had somehow done the right thing. The cemetery was on a hill and could only be reached by fording a low-water crossing, which was usually no problem. The front wheels of the hearse rolled right across, but, with the weight of the casket and the torrent of rainwater, the rear wheels sank in the soft white caliche clay and refused to move. "Schlunk" is the sickening sound I remember as we sank to the axles.

Now picture the scene: Six disgruntled businessmen, cajoled by their young pastor to do their Christian duty, alight from the limo in their best clothes and shoes. In a cold rainstorm, they slog a half mile up a muddy hill, carrying the casket of a guy they didn't like or respect to begin with, so their greenhorn preacher can do right by his calling. It was not a pretty scene, and their muttered exclamations were not from the Bible! "Let the dead bury their dead" might have been appropriate.

We got through it. We were soaked to the skin but we got through it, and "Showers of Blessing" never sounded quite the same to any of us after that.

They never let me forget that day, and for months my encounter with any one of those six men would begin with, "Well, preacher, what've you got in mind for us this afternoon?"

When our son, Mark, was a boy and would see me coming to the table on a weekday in my dark suit, white shirt, tie, and shined shoes, he would say, "Hey, Daddy's in his marryin', buryin', and riverboat gamblin' suit."

I wore it a lot in fifty-one years.

Chapter Four

A Funny Thing Happened on the Way to the Pulpit

When the bishop asks, "Are you willing to go where you are sent?" the response is "Yes," and it is one big yes followed by thousands of little yeses!

In our system, we are appointed to our ministry locations by the bishop, who represents the church which has trained and approved us for ministry. We go to places near and far, familiar and unknown, and make our way as pastors. It is an adventure of faith and can produce some truly hilarious experiences.

In this chapter, I share some of those with you.

I received my first pastoral appointment in 1956, after having served as a youth director for two years in a suburban church. I had finished my first year in seminary and was eager to experience the calling to which I had responded years earlier.

Annual Conference was held at First Church Dallas in those days, and on a warm June Sunday afternoon, Bishop William C. Martin was droning out the names of churches and appointees. He would pause after each church name to study the name of the person appointed, so as not to mispronounce some of the less familiar ones.

I was seated near the front on the main floor of the sanctuary, which was packed for the session. That was the era when appointments were made during the conference days, and many people did not know where they were being sent until the bishop read their names. Tension was high, curiosity at a fever pitch as we all listened intently. At one point the bishop read the name of a church and the appointee and then paused to study the next name. In that pause, a pastor's wife, sitting in the balcony, could be heard to exclaim, "Oh, no, not there!" all over the church.

I think she had her list of the ten worst appointments, and her husband had just been sent to number one!

Later, my name came out loud and clear: "Bailey Circuit, Tom Graves." Wow! I was appointed for the first time, and the adventure of pastoral service began.

Bailey, Gober, and Grove Hill were my three churches in southern Fannin County, Texas, and they provided me with some rare experience as I learned the ropes for the first time. I was eager and they were ready so we had a building project at each of the three churches in my first year! I got so engrossed in their life that I almost flunked out of seminary!

Grove Hill, my smallest church, had no running water, classrooms, kitchen, gathering space, or steeple. It was a pristine white frame church on a hillside overlooking a scenic valley, and its members loved it passionately.

We decided to build. Harold Sikes, a member, was a carpenter who had built other churches. He drew the plans, told us what to do, and we built classrooms, a fellowship hall, and a bathroom.

"We've got to have a steeple," I said to Harold toward the end of the other construction. So he designed a beauty. We built it on the ground and hired a small crane to lift it to the peak of the roof on a December Saturday so that we could anchor it properly.

A sleet storm moved in on Friday night, but the steeple was ready and the crane was there. We mounted the roof, bundled up with coats and caps and gloves, and watched through the downpour as our beloved steeple rose to its exalted position.

With icicles hanging from our ears and noses and eyelashes and frostbite threatening to set in on our frozen feet, we anchored our steeple. When we finally got inside around the stove to thaw, Harold looked at me and said, "Well, preacher, I guess we qualify as God's frozen people!"

Years later, when I was a district superintendent, Era, one of my small rural churches, was building a new fellowship hall and classrooms. On a November Saturday I went to participate in a wall-raising. It was great fun, and sure enough, it sleeted. Talk about déjà vu all over again!

Frozen, we walked over to the Baptist church where hot soup and coffee were ready, and the Baptist preacher said, "I heard you folks were cold and formal, but this is ridiculous!"

We thawed and rejoiced.

My second student appointment had two millionaires as members, and the church was in terrible disrepair. There was plenty of money out there, but it was all in their wallets, not the offering plates.

On my very first Sunday, Mrs. Peek, wife of one of the very wealthy members, stepped on a weak board of the front porch. It broke and gave way, and her leg went with it, breaking in several places.

With her help, we parlayed her injury into a total redo of the entire place. We had new carpet, new paint, a new porch with white columns, a lighted steeple, a new organ, brick sidewalks, a new parking lot, and a totally refurbished kitchen in the fellowship hall, appropriately named "Maverick Hall." We had people competing with each other to make the most ostentatious gift to the church rebuilding. It was not the kind of stewardship program I had in mind, but it sure worked!

I often thought, "What a fall into grace that was!"

After Linda and I married and she moved into the Bailey parsonage with me, the first funeral of the winter brought a new discovery. When the gas heaters warmed the church building, the wasps, nesting above the ceiling of the dome, began to unthaw and swarm in the sanctuary.

So, there I was, all robed up, trying to deliver a eulogy and some words of hope while dodging wasps and watching Linda, standing on the windowsills of the large stained-glass windows, spraying and swatting as many as she could and trying not to be a distraction. I seriously doubt that anyone there heard a word I said!

Later, the community was abuzz with the tales of the young pastor and his wife battling the wasps.

Among the yeses of being appointed is the willingness to live in the parsonage provided by the church.

Parsonage living is one aspect of pastoral ministry which demands flexibility. We lived in thirteen of them in seven full-time appointments. We helped build four new ones, and our experience ran the gamut from really great places to the not so great, from comfortable and convenient to flea-infested and leaky, from brand-new to one hundred plus years old.

We raised two children and a wide variety of pets, from dogs and cats to gerbils and hurt birds, from lab mice to various snakes. We even had a water moccasin in an aquarium on the patio, to the horror of our daughter, who would not take her boyfriends out there. The snake belonged to her younger brother, who collected hurt animals and nursed them to health.

Our second parsonage in particular stands out. As lay men and women from our former pastorate were helping us move in, Mr. Long, the church's volunteer handyman, appeared at the back door to reassure Linda and me that the leaks in the roof of the sixty-year-old house had all been repaired in preparation for our coming.

It was evident that the roof had been repaired when I

noticed the variety of composition shingle colors dotting the predominantly gray roof. The patches were shingles left over from other construction jobs and given away by the lumberyard! I was grateful, however, that we would be in the dry since it was January and the wettest winter in North Texas history.

I returned to the parsonage, which was next door to the church, on the first Sunday night in a driving rainstorm. After dripping dry in the kitchen, I heard "plink, plank, plonk, plunk" in quadraphonic from every room of the old house. It seemed Mr. Long had missed a few spots.

The house originally had two stories, but with smaller parsonage families and higher maintenance costs, the wisdom of the board dictated removing the second story and rearranging the first floor into a smaller residence. The wraparound victorian porch became two bedrooms and a bath, and the windows from the second story were used to enclose the rear of the porch into a walk-in closet, the interior of which was clearly visible from the parking lot! I didn't pick out my shirt in my skivvies because I never knew who was parking next to my closet!

We could hear rats in the attic doing acrobatics over the ceiling joists when things got quiet at night. So, one day I purchased large traps, climbed into the attic through a porch top entrance, baited them, and bided my time. That night, while in bed, I heard a clap! "Aha," I thought, "I got one." Then I heard the trap being dragged by the wounded rat to the wall by our bed. In the removing of the second story, no plates were put on the tops of the walls, and the rat fell down inside the wall by our bed and died.

We had to move out of the room, take boards off the

outside of the wall, and extract the rat body. After that, I went back into the dark attic and anchored the other traps.

It was, to say the least, an odorous experience!

The plumbing was home-done and interesting. The bathtub had an enormous drain. The pipe, which was free at the lumberyard, drained directly into the kitchen sink, so the bath water formed a soapy geyser on its way out of the house. On our first morning, as I was finishing my bath, Linda answered the front door and welcomed some women from the church who had brought goodies. At that moment, the geyser erupted in the kitchen and she exclaimed, "I don't know what that is!" One of the women, who had obviously been there before, said, "Oh, it's just someone taking a bath." To which Linda, frustrated, replied, "I think it's my husband." It was.

And then there were the floors. No two rooms sloped in the same direction, so we didn't need to throw the ball for the puppy. We just put it on the floor and let it roll! Other than that, it was a great house that was drafty and impossible to heat and cool, but the dining room was lovely with its strawberry-colored carpet which looked great with the lime-colored walls!

We were newlyweds and we didn't care.

My predecessor in that pulpit was an older man who retired from there. He was a rough-hewn guy who loved hunting and was a good outdoor cook, so he became the cook for the deer hunters during deer season. He liked it so much that he closed the church for two Sundays so he could go to the deer lease with the hunters and cook!

At my first appointment, John Hale had asked me on his front porch if I could preach. It seemed like a logical question for a greenhorn pastor, so I took it in stride. Then at my second church, no one seemed concerned about whether or not I could preach, but I was often asked, "Can you cook?"

Go figure.

At that same church, Sunday evening services were a thing of the past and the only thing happening in the building on Sunday nights was the youth program in Maverick Hall. One of the older men in the church complained regularly to me about the lack of worship on Sunday night.

"Would you come to church on Sunday night, Sam?" I asked him after the third complaint. "Oh, no," he replied, "my favorite TV program is on at that time [*Bonanza*, as I recall], but I just like driving by and seeing the lights on in my church on Sunday night."

I installed a timer in the sanctuary, and for one hour every Sunday night the lights were on. Sam was so happy that I never heard him complain again.

At the ranch house of one of the wealthy members, there was a pool and a tennis court. Some of the younger women played tennis weekly and then had cocktails by the pool.

After we moved in, these women invited Linda out for one of the outings and told her to bring her tennis racket, if she had one, and enjoy the company. What they didn't know was that she was a state champion tennis player in high school and played competitively in college. She took her racket, but her tennis shoes were worn out so she just wore a pair of old loafers.

She beat the local socialites so badly that day that they never asked her back for tennis!

With a starting salary, a new church to organize, and two small children, spending money was scarce. We had to save up for weeks for a simple night out.

On one occasion, we got a sitter and drove to downtown Dallas to see a movie at the Majestic Theater. We parked at Dunlap-Swain, the nearby parking garage, and started walking the block or so to the theater. Linda loved popcorn and she turned to me and asked, "Do we have popcorn money?" I acknowledged that we barely had enough to buy our tickets but that there might be some spare change in the car.

We raced back to the garage and were relieved to discover our car still waiting to be driven to an upper-level space. We opened up all the doors and scrambled, on hands and knees, looking under seat cushions and floor mats for loose change. Couples in expensive suits and mink stoles were staring as they walked past, having alighted from their Mercedes and Jaguars.

Oblivious, we counted the money and it was enough! Don't think I ever enjoyed a movie more or tasted better popcorn!

At our next appointment in Sherman, Texas, the church purchased a beautiful new parsonage, replacing the decaying old one, and one of the older women's Sunday School classes chose to buy the furniture for the living room. Linda accompanied them as they shopped for just the right combination and approved of their selection.

On the Saturday of delivery we were all at home. Mark, our five-year-old, was especially interested, since he considered these women his extra grandmothers. They arrived first, and soon the delivery truck pulled up in front of the new parsonage.

One by one, the pieces were put in place: the couch, end tables, lamps, coffee table, velvet chairs in the bay window, and other exquisite accessories, carefully chosen for this fine new place.

Mark watched with interest, sat in every chair and on every couch cushion, turned on all the lamps, and admired the entire scene. After appropriate approval, the president of the class signed the delivery invoice, accepted our thanks for their gift to the church and our home, and prepared to leave.

Mark, astonished, said as they approached the door, "Golly, we didn't even have to pay for it!"

Loving laughter ensued.

We moved the next June to a new parish, much to Mark's dismay. He loved our house, our neighborhood, his friends, and kindergarten. On the first Sunday in the new church, I was shaking hands and greeting people at the sanctuary door when a local doctor's wife approached me. "I taught Mark's Sunday School class today, and when I introduced him as the only newcomer, he responded with, "My name is Mark Graves and I left ninety-nine friends in Sherman, Texas!"

We often watched Walter Cronkite's newscast in the evenings, and Mark listened with awe at this older, wise man telling us "That's the way it is." We were watching *Laugh In* as a family one night and the cast was lampooning newscasters. They did a zany take-off on Cronkite's style and it was hilarious. Mark looked up, indignant, and proclaimed, "They shouldn't make fun of Walter Cronkite."

After all, some things are just sacred.

One Sunday we were honored to have the president of a major African-American college nearby as our preacher of the morning. Linda invited him to have lunch with us at the parsonage, which was immediately behind the church.

The college president was very black and dressed in an impeccable white suit. The lunch was delicious, and we were offered ice cream or watermelon for dessert. Our guest chose watermelon, which delighted Mark, since he thought of it as a major food group. Mark watched intently as our guest gently sliced the meat from the rind, disturbing neither, and then cut the meat into bite-sized pieces and ate each one, salted, with a fork. He didn't drip any juice on his white suit and enjoyed the whole thing immensely.

That night, Mark decided to try the new style. He took a knife, fan sliced carefully, but at an angle, with all the meat sliding off the rind onto the table. He picked it up, tried in vain to cut it into neat slices and, finally, in frustration, exclaimed, "This is ridiclious!" Thus a new word entered our parsonage vocabulary, because a lot of experiences in parsonages are "ridiclious!"

Linda loved candle trees, tropical beauties with gold blossoms on vertical stems surrounded by palmlike leaves. She planted some outside the kitchen windows, and since we had a warm winter with no frost, they grew quite tall and impressive.

November of the second year came, and the candle trees were in full bloom, brightening the west side of the house and the kitchen view with their extravagance. A frost was forecast for a mid month night, and Linda could not bear to give this beauty up. Knowing that the frost would surely take them, she took action.

So, here we were, this nutty couple in the parsonage of the dignified and historic First Church, doing the ridiculous. I was on the roof, freezing my buns off. Linda was on the ground, pinning bed sheets together, tossing them to me so that we could spread them over the tall candle trees and save them for a few more days.

People in passing cars were pointing and laughing, enjoying our apparent insanity. Frankly, I was willing to let Mother Nature have them, but love of the woman who loved the candle trees sent me to a number of unexpected places.

This time it was on the roof on a cold and windy night. At least, I thought, the pastor is high and lifted up for a few minutes.

Mark loved wheels and speed. Derby racers, go-carts, dirt bikes were all his cup of tea as a youngster. I think he had every racing car set available! I dreaded the day he turned sixteen and got a driver's license.

By then, however, Mark had rid his system of the speed addiction and purchased a 1970 International Scout, which would not do fifty-five miles an hour at top speed downhill. He named her "Tonto," after the most famous scout of oater fiction.

She was versatile and could be a four-seated enclosed car, a pickup, or an open vehicle. He worked on her so much that I remarked to him one night at dinner that I thought everything in her had been replaced but the driver.

One Wednesday when Linda's car was in the shop, I loaned her mine, thinking it would be fun to drive Tonto for a day. My morning appointment was a trip to a city an hour or so away for a meeting and lunch. Tonto was an open vehicle that spring, so the drive over was really nice and breezy. On the way back, a rain cloud opened up and it literally poured down.

So, there I was, in a suit and tie, crouched behind the vertical windshield, looking totally ridiculous to other motorists, who were smiling and pointing at the idiot who didn't have enough sense to come in out of the rain.

Ah, the joys of parenthood!

I was a skinny kid and my mother, a wonderful Irish cook, made a mission of trying to fatten me up. The mantra at mealtime was "Clean your plate and you can have dessert." I saw dessert as a reward for being a good boy. I think I still do, since I love sweets and reassure myself that, with all my foibles, I really deserve them.

Once after Linda and I had been married ten years, my mother called the parsonage and, after a brief greeting, said, "You sound thin. What is Linda feeding you?"

Sound thin! "Come on, Mom," I said, "you'd make a great Jewish mother!"

Ah, the joys of being an only child!

A friend of mine was pastor of a nearby church. The parsonage, next door to the church, had been a gift from a wealthy couple in the congregation. The wife of the couple, a local social climber, had a key and often came into the home provided for pastors and families without knocking.

One evening, my friend had just returned from hospital calls on a hot afternoon, and was showering before walking over to the church for a meeting. No one else was home, and while he was in the shower, the telephone rang. He padded, dripping, across the floor, to answer. He was drying his face, stark naked, and in walked the local dowager. He made no attempt to cover himself.

Taken completely aback, she stammered, "I knocked, I knocked." "Well," he said, "no one answered, did they?"

She left in a big hurry, muttering incoherently. Being a biblical literalist, she was probably thinking, "He could have at least worn a fig leaf!"

The pastor said it was difficult to make eye contact with her after that.

One of the biggest surprises of my pastoral life came a few months after we moved from Georgetown, Texas, where I had been pastor of First United Methodist Church for nine years. It was a truly wonderful and varied experience in a parish closely allied with Southwestern University, Texas' oldest college. Many faculty, staff, and students were members of the church, which also had a large contingent of ranchers, farmers, merchants, doctors, lawyers, and other professionals. I loved the challenge and the stimulation and so did my family.

One January morning at the new church, I received a very official-looking envelope from the president of the university. In his letter he informed me that the faculty and trustees of Southwestern had voted to honor me with a Doctor of Divinity degree at the spring convocation.

"Wow!" I thought, "Little Tommy Graves from Marked Tree, Arkansas, with a D.D.!"

The experience was made even more significant when I remembered that Southwestern never gave honorary degrees to pastors while they served there and very rarely to any who had moved on. It was a rare honor and I was excited.

I went home for lunch with the letter held tightly in my sweaty palm. Linda was preparing lunch. "Honey," I said excitedly, "Southwestern is giving me an honorary doctorate at the spring convocation."

She looked up from the stove and, after a moment, replied, "That's really nice, dear. Would you take out the garbage?"

That night I approached Mark, our high school freshman, who had grown up in Georgetown. He was doing homework by the fireplace. "Mark," I said, "we're going back to Georgetown in April for the spring convocation." "Really, Dad? Why?" he responded. "Because," I said proudly, "they're awarding me an honorary doctorate."

He looked up thoughtfully and said, "Oh, so you're gonna be the kind of doctor who can't do you any good, aren't you?"

"Well," I thought, "I am not calling my daughter, Lauren, at college to get put down one more time today. I just don't get no respect."

There is absolutely nothing like family to keep your feet planted firmly on the ground!

Family vacations are a source of refreshment, bonding, learning, and a lot of laughter. We were religious about vacations, and the early ones were camping trips because we liked them and couldn't afford many nights in a hotel or motel.

I remember some of these trips more vividly than others, and I share them with the hope that your own memory of good times will kick in as you read.

Our first family camping trip was to Ouray, Colorado, and the Amphitheater Campground, overlooking the town and in view of the San Juan chain of the Rockies. We were there in early June, and as we were eating breakfast on the picnic table in front of our tent camper, Mark said, "Look at those clouds, Daddy!" I looked down the valley and in the distance I could see snow clouds with the sun above them and snow falling out of them. It was a spectacular sight.

"I think it's coming our way," Mark remarked as we ate our bacon and eggs. Sure enough, the longer we watched this cloud patch, the closer it got, and before we could clear the table, everything, including us, was covered with a thick blanket of snow.

We retreated to the cover of the tent, had a family powwow, and decided our vacation needed, to coin a phrase, to go south, and so we did.

After Mesa Verde, we camped in Oak Creek Canyon, Arizona, just south of Flagstaff. It was the weekend of the Fourth of July and the big Indian powwow at the Rodeo Grounds in Flagstaff. We were the only Anglo family in the campground and got invited to wonderful campfires and dances.

Mark, almost three at the time, had refused to give up his nighttime bottle. Linda and I had told him he could bring one bottle on the trip, but if it got lost, that would be it. No more bottles.

We were seated high in the grandstand at the powwow, enthralled at the color and movement and wonderful variety of Native American dancing costumes and instruments. Mark got into the swing of things and stood on the bleacher seat, holding his bottle by the nipple and swinging it above his head to the beat of the music. Sure enough, out of his fingers it slipped, took one bounce, and rolled down the bleacher floors to the track at the edge of the arena.

Bewildered, he looked at his mother, who said, "That's it, little brave, your papoose days are officially over." He got the message and we never heard another word about a bedtime bottle after that!

Our favorite camping spot was Maroon Lake, south of Aspen, Colorado. In those days you could drive right in and seek a vacant designated spot. We always tried to get as close to the lake or to Maroon Creek as we could.

One year, Linda's parents, Mary and Paul, came up in their travel trailer and we all camped together.

On the first morning, Paul, Mark, and I found a nice big boulder by the lake and tried our hand at catching some mountain trout. We were one of many groups of fishermen dotted all around the lakeshore.

We tried flies, lures, worms, and meat, and, along with all the others, we caught nothing. Paul, never to be denied a catch, disappeared after about thirty minutes of failure. Later, he returned with a slab of Velveeta cheese and baited all our hooks with it.

Bingo! We got strikes and hauled in the trout for our

campfire supper. Mark caught the biggest one of all, and as the word spread about our bait, there was a major run at the cheese counter of the nearest grocery store!

Mark's string of fish was taller than he was, and his smile was not bad either.

One year we pulled our camper through Crested Butte, Colorado, and decided to traverse the pass on a newly graveled road to reach our rendezvous with other families at Crystal, a remote and beautiful campground. The trip over the pass turned out to be hazardous, treacherous, and downright scary, taking many hours and causing maximum anxiety. Shaken and frightened, we finally reached level ground, searching earnestly for other human beings.

After a turn in the road a small store with one gas pump appeared ahead. I pulled in and noticed two older bearded men in overalls and straw hats rocking back and forth on the legs of their cane-bottomed chairs. They were chewing tobacco and spitting at a coffee can several feet away, in a kind of unspoken contest to see who was the most accurate spitter. Our children were watching this scene with rapt attention.

I approached the porch. "What can I do for you, young feller?" one of the men said as he rocked back and prepared to spit at the can, which had been moved a foot or so farther.

"I need to know how to get to Crystal," I replied.

He reached his desired position, spit with gusto, and watched as his tobacco-laden saliva landed dead center in the can.

"Don't move an inch," he said, and took another chew for the next round.

We were there.

My friend Mike and I went with my son, Mark, the captain on a ship, to the waters of Guatemala, Belize, and Honduras. It was a great trip with a lot of kayaking and hiking.

In Belize there is a river called the Manatee River because the enormous mammals of that name swim in it and can be sighted on occasion. Along with a number of others, Mike and I kayaked up the river for several miles in search of the giant mammals. It was a scenic trip among the mangroves but, alas, no manatees.

On the way back down the river we were fifty feet or so behind an older couple, Ralph and Mamie, who were adventurous and seemed to love a challenge. We were watching them as we paddled, and suddenly their kayak careened into the air on the back of an adult manatee. They both flew out of the craft and landed in the river. We all gasped!

The staff Zodiac boat picked them up immediately, and I could see them laughing as they rode along, their kayak in tow. We headed back to the ship for the evening wrap-up of the day's activities and then dinner.

When I walked into the lounge, I spotted Ralph and Mamie at a table and went over to them. "How in the world did you two feel, being upended by a fifteen-ton mammal today?" I asked Mamie.

"Honey," she replied jauntily, "I had five kids in six years and nothing bothers me!"

Ralph snorted, "Aw, Mamie just lost her balance, that's all."

I think they became the poster couple for Manatee River kayaking!

Our first trip on a ship with our son Mark as the captain was the cruise up the Colombia and Snake Rivers in the Pacific Northwest. All the passengers spent the night in a hotel on the river at Portland, Oregon, and boarded after breakfast. We were in a large group of folks walking toward the ship, which was in the river below us.

Both Linda and I were eagerly watching the bridge for a glimpse of Mark in his captain's uniform. Sure enough, there he was, stripes and all, working with the officers and preparing for embarkation. Immediately behind us on the boardwalk was another couple, and as we walked along, we could hear the wife say, having spotted Mark, "Do you think that's the captain?" Her husband responded, "He's got the right number of stripes, so he must be the captain."

"My goodness, he surely looks young. Do you think he can run that ship?" (Mark was twenty-seven and the youngest captain in the industry at that time.) I almost had to put my hand over Linda's mouth to stifle the proud mother's response to her query, and quietly whispered that we should keep our identity to ourselves for Mark's sake.

That evening at the introductory session in the ship's lounge, Mark presented the officers, the crew, the naturalists, and the chefs to the passenger contingent and then said, "United States law requires that any deck officer on a U.S. commissioned ship must be at least twenty-one years old. Let me assure you that I do qualify, and if you have any questions, you can ask my parents, who are sitting at the back table."

So, in one fell swoop, he blew our cover!

There are eight locks and dams on the Columbia River, the first being the Bonneville. We reached there on our first day out.

There were two tugboats pulling large wheat barges ahead of us, but with radio communications between them, Mark, and the lock master, it was agreed that the tug boats and barges would go in first, leave a space for our ship, and then we would enter, thereby saving us an hour of waiting for the next opening.

Our cabin was on the bridge deck, and I was standing outside watching this whole operation as Mark steered the ship from the wing station on the outside of the bridge for better visibility.

The barges and tugboats were in place and we moved forward. The closer we got, the more it appeared to me that we were trying to park a tractor-trailer rig in a Volkswagen parking spot.

I yelled up to Mark, "Are we going to fit in there?" I got a patronizing look, and "Trust me, Dad, I've done this before." Appropriately chastised, I watched as we entered our spot with a wall of concrete on one side, a wheat barge in front of us, and a tugboat on the other side.

"How much clearance do we have?" I asked. "About a foot all around" was the response. He parked that ship in that spot, free floating and ready for the deck hands to throw the lines out to secure us. All the passengers were on deck to see this maneuver, and there was enthusiastic applause all around.

Later, an eighty-five-year-old woman, barely five feet tall, came up to the bridge and asked to see the captain. Looking up at him through her trifocals, she exclaimed, "Well, never again will I complain about trying to get my car into a parking space!"

Boarding, it was "How young he is!" Disembarking, it was "How good he is!"

If parental pride is a sin, I did a lot of sinning on that trip.

One summer Linda, Lauren, Mark, and I did a sailing trip through the Abacos, the outer islands of the Bahamas. Most of them are small keys and can only be reached by float plane or small boat. No cruise ships can navigate these waters, so tourism is limited.

As we sailed through these beautiful islands, we kept hearing from other sailors, "If you go to Green Turtle Key, be sure to stop at Miss Emily's Blue Bee Bar. It's a must for Abaco sailors."

We had planned to go to Green Turtle Key because Linda had read of a fine British artist who had a large home/gallery and studio there. Being an artist and interested in all kinds of art, she wanted to visit.

We anchored out, rowed in, and started hiking through the small village and up the hill to the artist's home. It was well worth the trip and he was there, hosting us and giving us a grand tour through his work.

On the way back down, we all agreed that we were ready for Miss Emily's, since it was August and we were soaked with perspiration and very thirsty. Miss Emily's is a simple island structure with a real Bahamian ambiance. We found a table and Miss Emily appeared to take our orders. "What's your specialty?" Mark asked. "Oh," she said, "the Goombay Smash. It has a little bit of everything blended just right." Mark ordered one and so did Lauren and I. We looked at Linda, who simply had no taste at all for alcohol, even wine at dinner. She thought a minute and then said, "If that's the thing to do on Green Turtle Key, bring me one too."

As we sipped, Mark, Lauren, and I were in an animated conversation and didn't notice that Linda, being very thirsty, was gulping her large drink down. By the time we looked over at her, her head was on the table and she was completely smashed on the Goombay Smash!

None of us had ever seen her this way before, so we got her up and managed to get her out the door for a picture showing her being held up by her children, with her head on Mark's shoulder and a faraway look in her eyes! We got her back to the sailboat, put her in a bunk, and didn't see her again until the next morning.

"Hey, Mom, how about another Goombay Smash?" became the taunt of the trip.

I wouldn't have missed it!

Okay, one more Linda vacation story.

We went to Nova Scotia to celebrate our fortieth anniversary. It was a fascinating trip back in time, especially Cape Bretton, the most like Scotland of all the settlements. Linda was into it all, the history, culture, music, art, brogues, festivals, and color. We immersed ourselves in their lives for two weeks and then headed back to our embarkation to Boston and home.

On our last night, Linda chose a bed and breakfast in an old Nova Scotian mansion, run by a retired Greek Orthodox priest. He was burly and bearded and presided over the most overly furnished, ornately decorated house I have ever seen. If there was a Greek or Nova Scotian artifact in existence, he either had it or a replica of it.

Linda engaged him in conversation about the Greek Orthodox tradition, which she had studied and was very informed about. He was so impressed with her interest that he confided that Saint Innocent was his patron saint. A long discussion of Saint Innocent ensued into the late hours of the evening.

The next morning, the priest had decided he could trust Linda with a look at one of his most precious treasures. He led her over to an ornate cabinet, unlocked it and retrieved a small reliquary, which is a repository for sacred relics. Enthralled at this marvelous cultural experience, she awaited eagerly as he opened the carved box, lined with velvet. There, to her shocked horror, was Saint Innocent's finger!

After all that esoteric discussion about comparative religions and traditions and practices, the ultimate revelation was a preserved finger! It took all her reserve to swallow the gasp that ensued.

The trip to the ferry was, as I recall, very, very quiet.

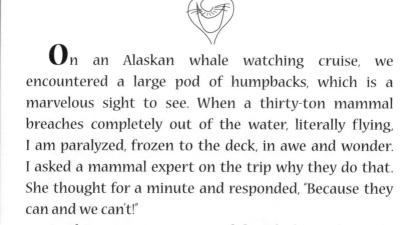

On an Alaskan whale watching cruise, we encountered a large pod of humpbacks, which is a marvelous sight to see. When a thirty-ton mammal breaches completely out of the water, literally flying, I am paralyzed, frozen to the deck, in awe and wonder. I asked a mammal expert on the trip why they do that. She thought for a minute and responded, "Because they can and we can't!"

On this trip, a very quiet and dignified British couple took it all in but said very little. On the morning we were in the midst of the whales, I was standing next to Miles, the Brit, and we watched in amusement as a professional photographer motored his small boat out and joined the whales for some pictures.

His tripod was set in the middle of his boat, and just as he would get all set to snap, the humpbacks would disappear and reappear at the stern. Frustrated, he would reverse his direction, get set again, and they would be gone, to surface again on his port or starboard side. It was as if they were playing games with this cameraman and enjoying it. This went on for some time, and his frustration was evident, even from several hundred yards away on the top deck of the ship.

Just when his anger at these uncooperative mammals

seemed to reach its peak, Miles cupped his hands beside his mouth and shouted in his most clipped British accent, "Do you have any Gray Pupon?"

I will not describe here the obscene gesture he got from the cameraman!

Use your imagination.

Chapter Five

O Come to the Church in the Wild World

It has been said that "Jesus came bringing the kingdom, and what we got was the church!"

These stories seemed to demand their own category, since they didn't quite fit in the previous chapters. They recount things that could only happen in local church life and in pastors' lives, when the circumstances, chemistry, and karma combine in just the right combination with the tides and the alignment of the planets.

They are definitely not from the age of Aquarius!

✝

I was finishing my year of postgraduate study at the University of Edinburgh, Scotland, when the call came from my District Superintendent back home. I had expected to be appointed to the same or some other small town church for my first full-time appointment. To my surprise, he said, "Tom, we want you to start a new church in southwest Oak Cliff in Dallas." I was thrilled at the challenge and opportunity that appointment presented and said "Yes" immediately.

The church site was a five-acre corner adjoining a large subdivision of starter homes. Settled in a rented parsonage, we set out to find people who would come to our first worship service on July 5 in our rented school auditorium, which would be our church home for three years.

We were almost a monolith of young families with first jobs, first babies, and first mortgages. We provided a nursery in our home, but many parents preferred to bring their toddlers with them to worship.

I became accustomed to preaching to a background of screaming children who stood up on the theater seats of the auditorium and became trapped as the whole apparatus folded up and entrapped their little bodies. When this occurred, adults from nearby seats would join the parents in extricating the child, offering words of comfort and, sometimes, first aid!

We had more children than adults, so it was rarely quiet.

I moved to an older, more formal, and more self-consciously dignified congregation after seven years at Saint Andrew's. On one of my first Sundays at Key Memorial Church in Sherman, a babe in arms cried out once during the sermon. At the door, a middle-aged, well-dressed, and very officious woman took my hand and said, "Oh, Pastor Graves, I do hope that rowdy child didn't disturb you in our lovely service."

My unexpressed thought was, "Honey, if you knew where I'd come from, you would realize how ridiculous that sounds." However, being the kind pastor, I said, "My dear, it was music to my ears."

I don't think she got it.

✝

We had a lot of bright ideas about how to do church at Saint Andrew's without our own building. Those of us who had gone to church before simply took many things for granted. Hymnals, communion sets, musical instruments, literature, and dozens of other things had been provided for us by those who came before us.

But, at Saint Andrew's, it was up to us to improvise as we started from scratch. In our collective wisdom, we decided to have a summer revival, so we rented a large tent, chairs, and a small organ. We set up near our lighted billboard on the church site and plugged our lights in to that power source.

One concern was protecting the property during the late hours of the night, so some of the men took a night apiece and slept on a cot in the tent, just to be safe. Ivy and Nell Williams were a middle-aged couple with no children. They were very close, like two sides of the same coin, but Ivy, faithful guy that he was, volunteered for a night of church sentry duty.

What Ivy didn't know was that there was a small ranch less than a mile down the hill to the west and the owner's hobby was raising peacocks. If you have ever heard a peacock's sound, you know it is a penetrating screech, which comes to human ears as "Help! Help! Help!" The rancher had dozens of the beautiful birds, and once one of them started, the others chimed in and there was a din of "Help! Help! Help!"

Ivy was terrified at the sound, jumped up, drove home in his pajamas, awoke Nell, and insisted that she get a cot and come stay with him in the revival tent. She did and she assured him that they were just peacocks, not dozens of women in dire distress.

I don't remember their scaring the hell out of anyone during the revival services. But, then, you never know, do you?

Another one of our brilliant moves in public relations/evangelism was to stage a living nativity each night on our property. We chose the week prior to Christmas and began collecting the component parts months in advance.

We had donkeys, a couple of cows, sheep, and even a couple of camels, loaned to us by the peacock rancher, who was addicted to exotic animals. Those who could design and sew worked diligently on the costumes for shepherds, wise men, Mary, Joseph, the Baby Jesus—a real infant, by the way—and, of course, one angel.

We were pretty proud of the authenticity of our set, which was an above-the-ground cave designed by one of our laymen. The whole thing was wonderfully lighted, with the angel appearing at the appropriate time above the cave, carefully perched on a ladder, disguised as a cloud. And there was appropriate recorded music. Man, I'm telling you, it was impressive as the dickens!

On the second night, cars began to come by in large numbers because visitors from the night before had spread the word that there was a really live nativity right here in our own neighborhood. We were so proud.

That night, however, one of donkeys seemed restless, tugging at the rope held by the nine-year-old shepherd. Suddenly, something bit him—the donkey, not the shepherd—on the rump. He pulled away from the shepherd, stepped forward, and bit Mary on the arm. We closed the show for that night and rushed Mary to the hospital. The entire human cast and their families were in hot pursuit. Imagine the consternation of the doctor and nurses on duty in the emergency room when they surveyed this ragtag group of kings and shepherds accompanying the injured maiden.

"This is Mary," Joseph said, "and she's been bitten by a donkey!"

It was a Christmas Eve night to remember in the emergency room at Methodist Hospital!

Mary dutifully resumed her role the next night with a large bandage on her arm and a baby in her arm. This production was more realistic than we had planned.

✝

Money was always in short supply at Saint Andrew's. The offering was counted carefully several times, including the pennies. The checkbook was kept in a locked drawer in our temporary office building, a ten-by twenty-foot metal structure which we bought and modified during our first year in the school building.

One morning, I got a call from a shoe store asking me to please come and cover the hot check on my church which they had received several days before. Puzzled, I went and saw that the check had a bogus signature but was our imprinted check. The bank, of course, would not honor it, since our treasurer did not sign it.

When I returned to the church, after a sincere apology to the store manager, I had other calls from other merchants all over Dallas with the same complaint. I soon discovered that pages at the back of the checkbook had been stolen, and salary checks had been written with professional check-protectors and cashed by persons claiming to work for the church.

We were victims of a check-stealing ring, and our public image was suffering a major blow as these merchants had to eat the loss. It was embarrassing, to say the least. We took a special offering to repay the merchants and soon the thieves were apprehended in a suburban residence several miles away.

When asked at their trial if I had anything to say, I quoted my Grandmother Graves, who often told me, "Be sure your sins will find you out." Then I added, "When this is over, come on to church with us and find out how rich you can be without stealing from God. Grace is free and so is acceptance and forgiveness. Come and see."

My church treasurer, who accompanied me to the courthouse, burst my self-righteous bubble with "Man, I never heard you sound so pious! I guess I'll have to treat you with more respect, most holy one."

The halo was short-lived.

✝

One of our bright ideas, after moving into our own facilities, was to have movie/discussion nights on Wednesdays during the summer. We would choose a film, view it together, and then break into small groups to discuss the moral and spiritual issues and questions this film evoked in us. It was a very popular program.

Toward the end of the summer, we decided to order a biblical film as an example of Hollywood's portrayals of the stories of our faith. *King of Kings*, a contemporary remake of the old silent film by the same name, had swept the country, so we got a copy and the place was packed.

We eagerly awaited seeing this full-color extravaganza about Jesus right there in our own sanctuary. The place was packed with members and visitors. It was a big deal for a summer Wednesday.

The film arrived late, so there was no chance to preview it before the public screening. Dave Adams, our projectionist for the night, had the lights dimmed and was preparing to flip the switch when a man, who had obviously had too much to drink, walked in off the street, came down the aisle, and took a vacant seat near Dave.

The film began and we were aghast! It was not the new *King of Kings*; it was the original silent film, with exaggerated gestures, melodramatic facial expressions, and very strange music. The words were mouthed by the cast, and the text appeared, somewhat blurred, at the bottom of the screen.

The crowd sat in embarrassed silence. Dave didn't know what to do and neither did I. What a mess! What a disappointment! What a bad film!

In the silence, the drunk man leaned over to Dave and said loudly, "Hey, buddy, turn up the volume, I can't hear a thing they're saying."

That broke the tension. We all laughed, relaxed, and took a trip back in filmmaking, grateful that progress had been made since then.

The drunk man slept through the whole thing!

✝

From the beginning, we had good music at Saint Andrew's. Donna Ruth, our volunteer choir director, saw to that. She simply would not allow swing tunes, bad lyrics, or lousy theology to be sung by her choir. "Jazz for Jesus just doesn't go here!" And that was that.

In that era, there were a number of gospel quartets and groups with television programs, singing the very songs Donna Ruth would not accept. One particular group was very popular throughout the South and Southwest. They wrote many of their own songs and published their own songbook, used in many churches, but not at Saint Andrew's!

Their pianist was a flamboyant showman. Liberace had nothing on this man. He dressed to the nines, had a dentist-enhanced smile, and did runs and flourishes with all the gestures of the finest maestro in the largest orchestra in the world. His name was well known, and he made a bundle playing jazz for Jesus. We all knew what Donna Ruth, a fine pianist herself, thought about this guy!

At a choir Christmas party one year in the home of the Holders, choir members with a grand piano, the early conversation was somber and subdued. As we munched on appetizers, we grieved over the early death of one of our young adult members who was a staunch supporter of the choir. It was not a very celebrative evening.

Donna Ruth, who always had a keen sense of the moment, sensed the mood, went to the grand piano, put on a pink feather boa, pasted a fake smile on her face, raised both hands in a flourish, did a full-keyboard run, and played the jazziest medley of Stamps-Baxter songs any brush arbor revival ever heard! It was incredibly funny and totally out of character for our beloved director. The somber mood was broken. We celebrated life and not death as we regained our ability to laugh at the absurd and love and enjoy each other.

We sang a lot of carols. We weren't quite ready for prime time, but we made a very joyful noise!

There was a Swedish Annual Conference in Central Texas at one time. The services were in Swedish, and the traditional Swedish church customs were observed by the many immigrants who settled in the area.

As a result, Georgetown had two United Methodist Churches diagonally across the intersection from each other—First Church, where I became pastor, and Saint John's, the former Swedish Church, which now spoke English and only observed one big Swedish Christmas tradition.

On the corner across from both churches was a beautiful colonial mansion owned and occupied by Grogan and Dorothy Lord, a millionaire couple who were members of First Church. Anyone could tell you there were two United Methodist Churches in Georgetown and the Lord lived in between!

Pedro was our church custodian and a fine one. He kept the church so clean and shining that he would have been very happy if it had been a museum and uncluttered all the time. He liked to "dust the audience," and any time you told him you needed him for a certain chore, his response was "I'm valuable."

Pedro was a successful pig farmer who also cleaned First National Bank and several other buildings. He was so knowledgeable about livestock in general that Grogan Lord would not buy or sell cattle unless Pedro told him the market was right. Grogan often confided in me that he had made a million dollars following Pedro's advice.

His English may not have been the best, but his intelligence was far above average.

Just goes to show that you can't tell a Pedro by its cover.

✝

One of the most beloved curmudgeons ("crusty old men:" Webster) I have known was Billy Bob. He was president of First National Bank and the chairman of the finance committee at First Church.

I banked at First National and, after taking care of my own business, would always go over to Billy Bob's desk for a short visit. He insisted on having his desk in the middle of the lobby so that he could see all the customers as they came and went.

One season I got so busy with church, family, and community that spare minutes were hard to come by so I did my banking at the drive-in window. Billy Bob's feelings were hurt, and he fussed at me for not coming inside. On my next visit to the lobby, he crooked his index finger at me, motioning me to come over to his desk. I did, and an hour later, I got back to the church. It seems he had stored up all the things he wanted to tell me and gave me the whole load. I did my banking inside from then on.

Billy Bob was so habitual that you could set your clocks by his walks down University Avenue to work. He and his wife sat in the very same pew and seats every Sunday. They came in and exited by the same door and never varied from that route on the north side of the sanctuary.

When his daughter's wedding rehearsal night came, I reminded the bride and father that they would process down the south aisle and recess out the north aisle. Billy Bob, then in his sixties and a lifelong member, looked at me and said, "I've never been up the south aisle."

One communion Sunday I asked everyone to return to a different part of the sanctuary after their time at the chancel to symbolize the difference forgiveness makes in our lives. We all watched Billy Bob, who was very frustrated that someone else took his seat before he got back to it. He sat as close as he could to his own sacred spot for the remainder of the service.

One wonderful financial campaign we actually oversubscribed the budget with our pledges. This had not happened before in anyone's memory, and it was the talk of the church. I was delighted beyond belief, since we really needed some breathing room for special missional projects. I eagerly anticipated the finance committee meeting and the report of the campaign committee, sure that we would take a few moments to celebrate and rejoice.

As soon as the report of the over-the-top pledge was complete, Billy Bob cleared his throat and grumbled, "Well, I think the budget was just too small."

My first thought was "Bah, humbug!"

My secretary, Alice, was a treasure. She, as I did, came from a journalistic family and career. A Canadian, she worked well with deadlines, and we always had them in the church office. She was meticulous and would spend hours making sure the bulletins and newsletters were neat, error free, and free of bad punctuation. She was very proud of all our publications, and there was rarely a flaw.

Our Youth Director was a college student name Joe, a multitalented and highly energetic young man who influenced many teenagers with his teaching, his wit, and his example.

Joe was very creative in many ways, including drawing. He would breeze into the church office on a Wednesday afternoon, grab two mimeograph stencils and a stylus, sit down at a typewriter, and intermittently type and draw until both stencils were filled with stuff that teenagers would see and read. After thirty minutes of creating, he would run off the copies he needed and dash out to get his fraternity brothers to fold them so he could have them in the mail by the next morning.

Slow and meticulous Alice would watch the whole procedure and sigh, "That is just disgusting!"

✝

Once, when our District Superintendent, who was a former pastor, blew into the office with smiles, handshakes, and much verbiage with no content, the office somehow seemed filled with hot air. On his departure, we enjoyed a few moments of silence, broken by Alice's comment, "You know, Tom, he's solid veneer. I mean, deep down, he's shallow!"

Alice may not have been from wonderland, but she always had the right words.

✝

One summer, a group of men from the community organized a deep sea fishing trip in the Gulf of Mexico. They invited me to go along, and I accepted.

We boarded our sixty-foot trawler at Port Arkansas and set out at midnight for the red snapper beds. About dawn we arrived and began baiting our hooks with smelly squid. Just about the time the snappers began to bite, we were part of a large Gulf swell with fifty-foot waves. The Coast Guard called in all small craft, so we turned around and headed back to the coast.

It was a five-hour trip and it was rough, very rough. I knew if I could see the horizon I could avoid seasickness, so the high school principal and I stayed on deck with our arms wrapped around the handrail on the outside of the cabin.

All the other men and their sons were inside, and many were very sick. They would watch the sea out those stern windows where I stood. I did fine for a while, but the smelly squid sliding all over the deck, the salt water splashing all over us, and the increasingly violent motion finally got to me.

I rushed to the rail and lost all the food I had digested and some that I hadn't.

At that point I heard Billy Tubbs, the university basketball coach, yell, "Oh man, we're in trouble now; the preacher's on his knees at the rail."

I think my prayer was "Come, sweet death."

Land never before or since has looked so good to me. When we finally arrived and I got onto terra firma, I knelt and kissed the ground.

I was not the only one.

✝

The Lay Witness Mission was one of many spiritual fads to sweep into many local churches in my lifetime. The idea was that a team of deeply spiritual lay men and women from other churches would come for several days, give their oral testimonies, and meet with small groups for new spiritual experiences. The primary focus was the witness of laity to other laity. Thence the name, "Lay Witness Mission."

One of the experiences involved was called the "Jesus Chair." In this setting, members of the church would take their turn in a chair placed in the center of the circle of lay witnesses and confess their sins for forgiveness, cleansing, and absolution.

A number of people had unburdened themselves of various small sins in one particular group, when a young woman's turn came up. She was the church secretary, well known to all in the group and a somewhat sainted figure at good old First Church. She began much as other occupants of the Jesus Chair had done, and her sins sounded pretty mundane to the circle.

Then, without warning, she burst into tears and sobbed, "I'm having an affair with the pastor."

[Let me be clear, this was not my church!]

The stunned silence was broken by the voice of one of the men in the circle who said, "Now that's a lay witness!"

What's in a name? In this case quite a bit.

✝

Restoring and refurbishing a one-hundred-year-old antique gem of a sanctuary is a challenge full of adventures. We had a few at First Church Corsicana.

While the sanctuary was under reconstruction, we moved the morning worship services into our fellowship hall. To accommodate everyone, we asked those with last names beginning with letters from A to M to come to the early service, and N to Z to the late one, with adjustments for special needs.

People were very cooperative, and we worked hard to make the space as worshipful as possible. Banners, communion table, candlesticks, brass cross, hymnals, and bulletins all reminded everyone that we were, indeed, in church. An organ was already there, and there was room for the choir, the pastor, and the associate on the small stage.

The chairs were vintage 1920s, when the building was built. They were single plywood folding chairs and had served well for many years.

To make the space even more festive, the choir, acolytes, and ministers robed and processed down the center aisle during the first hymn. I could see the worship committee beaming as we mounted the stage and finished the hymn with a flourish. We had truly made this makeshift sanctuary work! I was the first person to the improvised pulpit, giving the welcome and the opening prayer. In the silence that ensued, I sat down and my chair collapsed or exploded, depending on your perspective, and I landed in the lap of an ample soprano in the first row of the choir.

Well, so much for formality in the Fellowship Hall! After that, it all seemed much more relaxed and normal.

✝

The sanctuary thermostat was on a large column beside the chancel area, clearly visible to all.

People who felt either hot or cold felt free to walk up to it and make the adjustment in the temperature to suit their own body thermostat. It was confusing and not very efficient.

With the installation of the new central heating/cooling system, we moved the thermostat into a hallway foyer in an inconspicuous place, where, hopefully, only the ushers knew the location.

We decided, however, to leave the original one in place, even though it was disconnected.

Sure enough, people still went to it, made their own adjustments, and returned to their seats feeling so much cooler or warmer because of their direct actions. The relief was evident on their faces. Funny how interconnected our mental and physical systems really are.

We fessed up to the congregation after a few weeks of the ruse. I'm not sure they ever trusted that committee completely after that.

✝

We had a fine Youth Director who related wonderfully to the many teenagers in the congregation, including my son, Mark. Sometimes on an outing, however, his judgment was not the best you could imagine.

One Wednesday night, after a lengthy committee meeting, I got a call at my office from the local police station. The captain asked me to come down because he had our Youth Director and our entire youth group in custody! I hadn't expected to do jail ministry that night, but down to the police station I went.

There, slinking behind bars in a large holding cell, was our entire youth program! It seems our director thought it would be fun to rearrange the letters on the marquee of the drive-in theater at the edge of town to read, "Bring your youth to First United Methodist for a great time!"

A passing motorist notified the police and they all ended up in the pokey.

Now, I believe in good advertising, but that's going a little too far. We got them off with a warning and a promise to behave within the law.

There were red faces and relieved parents all around.

✝

Several years later, we welcomed Will, our new associate, a first-year seminary student and a very committed young man. As he was moving into his office, I reminded him to disarm the alarm system before he entered the building at night to avoid a lot of noise and a call from the police.

As he was moving his books into his office one night, his arms were full of boxes and he forgot to disarm the system. The police called me at home to report a burglar in the building who claimed he was a new staff member. I went down and saw Will in dirty jeans, T-shirt, and sneakers, flanked by two of our local policemen. He looked scared, embarrassed, and pathetic.

"Does this young man really work for your church?" the officer asked.

Realizing I'd never get a better chance to use this line, I said, "Officer, I've never seen him before in my life."

The look on Will's face was priceless. He was incredulous, stunned, and bewildered.

I came clean, and everyone laughed but Will, who looked at me with suspicion for several weeks.

However, he never forgot to disconnect the alarm after that.

✝

A rapidly growing suburban church was a new challenge. I had never belonged to one, much less been its pastor. It was First Church Plano, with a big staff and a far-flung program and I plunged in.

One sunny Sunday morning, as I was visiting with the choir at the back of the sanctuary, preparing for the processional down the aisle, I noticed a woman—a visitor—walking past with a coffee cup in her hand. It was not unusual for a worshiper to arrive absentmindedly at worship with a cup left over from the fellowship time between services, so I thought nothing of it and turned back toward the choir.

In a few moments the music of the organ prelude was joined by a ranting female voice telling the assembled congregation that they were going straight to hell for their wicked ways and listing the dire consequences of their blatant unbelief. I looked up to see the woman I had greeted a few minutes before, standing in the top row of the choir loft, eyes blazing, arms waving, and admonitions laced with profanity spouting from her mouth.

The incident occurred during a time of well-publicized shootings in churches near and far, so my congregation was tense from the first word shouted, and became more fearful and agitated with each awkward moment. In the vernacular, "Butts were clenching all around!"

The organist didn't know whether to soften or increase the volume to drown her out, stop playing altogether, or duck under the bench until the verbal storm blew over. Our head usher, John, rushed up the choir loft steps and began trying to reason with this self-appointed prophet. She continued unabated so Linda joined John to add her persuasiveness to the nondialogue. It did no good, so I transversed the long aisle in a hurry, robe and stole flapping, mounted the steps, and pitched in.

"What seems to be the problem here?" I asked. "God told me this morning that I was supposed to preach at this here church and that's what I'm gonna do," was her response. "Is that right?" I replied. "God told me four years ago to preach here every Sunday, and he didn't let me know you were coming today, so you must have the wrong church!"

I don't know who looked more startled at my pronouncement, John, Linda, or the strange visitor.

I could see she was a little off balance at that point, so I added, "And if you don't agree to come down quietly, I'm sure the fire department will be glad to help you when I call them within the next minute." She did come down and we learned that she was bipolar, that she was off her medication, and that the coffee cup contained her fourth bourbon of the morning.

Linda and John both acknowledged that, until that morning, they never heard me claim to have heard the clear and distinct voice of God giving me specific instructions. I refused to explain and received a new title from that day forward.

The next day, the nameplate on my door read: Dr. Tom Graves, pastor/exorcist!

Smart aleck laypeople. What do they know?

✝

I was a regular on the list for jury duty in Collin County, and that, too, was an education and an adventure. On one occasion, the case was a capital murder offense, committed at a convenience store just a few blocks from the church.

Jury selection is a somber, humorless, and intense business. It entails waiting and waiting to take the stand and field questions from both attorneys, and then waiting some more for the decision about those who would go on to the next phase of questioning.

The judge in this case was a member of my congregation, and I had presided at his daughter's wedding the previous June. We never acknowledged each other during the proceedings, and the day dragged on.

Finally, around five o'clock, I was still there, one of the fifteen remaining candidates for the panel. I took the stand and the defense attorney asked me, among other things, if I knew any of the principles in the case—the accused, family members, the victim, family members, the other attorneys, and on and on and on.

Exasperated at all my negative answers, he asked, "Do

you know anyone in this courtroom?"

"Yes, I know Judge Roach," I replied. "How do you know Judge Roach?" he asked, sensing a crack in my integrity. "He's a member of my congregation," was the honest response. "Would your relationship with Judge Roach in any way prejudice you in deliberating this case?" he continued.

I simply couldn't resist. The bored exhaustion in that room was palatable, and there hadn't been a chuckle, much less a laugh, all day, so I used my best line: "Why, no, Congressman Sam Johnson is a member of my congregation and that hasn't made me a Republican!"

Judge Roach rolled his eyes, and the other potential panelists laughed when they realized the truth of the statement and its potency in a predominantly Republican county. They all thanked me for saving the day from total gloom and doom.

I was not chosen for the jury.

There were several suggestions from others in the room that I might consider becoming a stand-up comic.

I don't think so.

✝

Toward the end of the eighth challenging, fruitful, and happy year of my pastorate at First Plano, the bishop called and asked me to come to his office. I had not made a habit of visiting bishops and knew this was something important. I had heard rumors of appointments I might be offered and had my defenses all ready to decline them and stay put.

The visit was very cordial and then he asked me to join

his cabinet and become superintendent of the Sherman-McKinney District! It was totally unexpected and I was flabbergasted.

I had sworn on all that was holy to me that, no matter what roles I was asked to play in our appointive system, I would do it willingly, EXCEPT be a District Superintendent. I was a pastor and I loved being a pastor, and that was that. I had turned this opportunity down once before to another bishop and thought that settled it.

The problem was that I really liked this bishop and had always felt strong spiritual ties with him, with his goals and values, with his style and candor. He was my kind of guy. AND he asked me to go to my favorite district of the eight in which I had served. I was challenged and told him I would think about it over the weekend, talk to God and Linda (not necessarily in that order!), and call him on Monday morning.

Driving back to the church in a stunned daze, I called Linda at home. "What did the bishop want?" she asked.

"He wants us to go to the Sherman-McKinney District."

"What did you tell him?" she pushed further.

"I told him I would talk to you and God and let him know."

"What do you think you're going to do?"

"I think I'm going to do it," I said very slowly. There was a very long wifely silence from the woman who had heard me swear, vow, pledge, and commit never to do this.

Then she said, "You've got to be kidding."

She packed, we sold the only house we'd ever owned, and we went.

It was a great trip. I'm not kidding!

✝

Esther Peck came up to me on my first Sunday as interim pastor at First Church McKinney, after retirement. I was visiting in the congregation before worship and she introduced herself.

I told her that I was the new pastor. She looked to be about sixty-five and was barely five feet tall. She looked up at me, poked my shoulder with her index finger, and said, "Honey, we're the church. You're just the shepherd."

I responded, "Sister, you just preach that gospel all over the place, because that is exactly the truth!"

We became fast friends and I learned that she was ninety-two! At lunch one day she said, "Tom, why don't you quit what you're doing for a while and come with me?" "Where are you going, Esther?" "I'm going cross-country skiing in Vermont!" was the response.

She did, and brought back great pictures of the adventure. "Esther, if I can be like you, I'll go to ninety-two."

✝

Later, I was visiting Vona Smith in an assisted living facility. She had just celebrated her one hundred and first birthday. "Vona, happy birthday," I said. "I've got a birthday coming up in a few days." "How old will you be?" she asked. "Seventy-three" was my response. She patted me on the knee and said, "Tom, you're just a kid." "Say that again, Vona," I responded. "That sounds really good."

✝

Both of these encounters reminded me of my fortieth birthday years earlier. It was a Sunday and my family gave me a big red button with white letters that read, "Be kind to me. I'm forty today."

As I stood on the porch of the education building, shaking hands with those coming in to Sunday School, Gladys Whitcomb came up the walk on the arm of her husband, Dudley. She spotted my button but couldn't read it from the bottom of the steps. She stepped up close, read it, and said, "Big deal. I'm eighty-seven!"

Just simply puts it all in perspective, doesn't it?

✝

And then there was the pastor who asked an older woman in his church if she believed in the hereafter. "I certainly do" was the indignant response. "Every time I walk into a room, I think, "What am I here after?"

I know exactly how she feels.

✝

One spring Sunday I was the guest preacher at a church whose pastor was on a trip with his wife and children. I spent Saturday night with my daughter and grandchildren and then drove over to the church where I was to preach both services. As I was getting dressed and digging in my overnight bag, I discovered, to my dismay, that I had forgotten to pack my dress shoes. All I had were my sneakers. Too late to go home for shoes, so I wore my suit and sneakers.

It got a good laugh at the early service, and comments like, "That's probably closer to what Jesus would wear than polished leather."

Shaking hands in the pews before the late service, I was robed and stoled and came across a row of teenage boys. As I introduced myself, one of them looked down and exclaimed, "Hey, man, neat shoes!" and stuck out his foot with the exact same shoe on it.

I was in with a hard-to-reach bunch of teenage boys.

Maybe I'll wear sneakers in the pulpit exclusively from now on!

One of the fringe benefits of being clergy and an amateur sailor was being invited by the commodore to become chaplain of the sailing fleet at Lake Texoma. One of the duties was the blessing of the fleet at the annual regatta in the spring. It had become an international event, with more than a hundred sailing vessels participating. The race itself was beautiful and exciting, with spinnakers flying, flags waving, and crews dressed in brilliant colors.

As the boats came out of the marina, I stood on the bow of a cruiser at the entrance to the larger lake and gave each one a blessing with outstretched arms. I wore jeans, deck shoes, T-shirt, and a nautical stole.

Sailors are notoriously superstitious and are all careful to come by for the blessing before sailing out to the starting point of the race. To many of them I look like a priest, so as they sail by, glasses are raised, caps donned, and the sign of the cross made with reverently bowed heads.

"Thank you, Father!" is often shouted as the boat passes.

The first year I did the blessing, I remember thinking, "Wow, I don't get this kind of homage from my Methodist parishioners. Maybe I'm working for the wrong bunch!" Perhaps, I mused, if I started wearing a clerical collar. No, probably not. I don't even like neckties!

Oh well, back to the nitty-gritty give-and-take of the real world.

✝

Betty Taylor is the person who facilitated my book-writing career and became my pro bono agent, having spent years as a publisher's representative. Betty is a very meticulous person and wants everything just right, especially in my books. I respect this, and am a better writer because of her.

When my first book, *From My Perspective*, was shipped, I drove out to the warehouse to get a glimpse of the finished product. As I cut open the box on the tailgate of my truck and reached in, I asked myself, "Graves, what's the big deal? You've been handling this material for more than a year. It's been edited and reedited, designed, proofed, and examined in a dozen ways. Why are you excited?"

I pulled out a copy and looked lovingly at it, thinking, "Hey, it's a book! It's not a manuscript anymore, it's a book.

It's got fingers and toes and eyes and ears." I had been told it was a kind of birth experience from other authors. On the way to Betty's house to give her some copies, I drove with the book on the seat of the passenger's side, looking admiringly from time to time at this wondrous creation.

I called Betty. "Tom," she answered. "Betty, we just can't sell this book." "Why not!" she said in a panic. "Are some of the pages upside down? Are they out of order?" and she proceeded through a long list of things she had seen go wrong through the years between manuscript and book.

I just let her go until she finally fell silent, and then I said, "It's just too pretty."

"I am going to kill you!" was the response.

She didn't and I'm still writing.

✝

I returned to Marked Tree, Arkansas, my hometown, to review my second book, *From Marked Tree to Red 'Arc*, at an annual luncheon to benefit the local library. It was my first trip back to this village of 2,700 people, and some things had changed.

After a visit at the church with the women in the kitchen preparing the luncheon, and a talk with the pastor, I drove to my father's old newspaper office to peruse the files from years of my childhood. I found wonderful columns he wrote during my childhood and copied them for my grandchildren.

After several hours there, I went to Home Street to see our old house. It had shrunk considerably since my childhood! Then I drove down to the banks of the Saint Francis River, one of my favorite haunts as a boy. I got some lunch and headed over to Mary Ann Arnold's house.

Mary Ann was the person who invited me and was my hostess for the afternoon and night. Her mother and my mother were fast friends when I was a child.

I rang her doorbell. She appeared and said, "I'm so glad to see you, Tom. I heard you were in town and went to the church to visit the ladies and the pastor. Then you spent time at the Tribune office and the McGills spotted your truck on Home Street by your old house. After that you went to the river for a while before lunch."

I laughed and said, "Mary Ann, it's so nice to learn that no matter how much some things have changed, the Marked Tree grapevine is still faster than the speed of light."

The word around Marked Tree was, "Tommy Graves is back in town."

And so he was. And it was very, very good.

EPILOGUE
The Tale of the Cat

A beautiful white Persian cat arrived on our deck shortly after Linda and I moved to Red 'Arc Farm in May of 2001. We learned she had belonged to a neighbor who was moving away. She decided not to go, and proceeded to adopt us as her new family.

After observing her for a few weeks, I named her "Cleopatra, Queen of the River," since we live on the Red River, which separates Texas from Oklahoma, and her demeanor was definitely regal. Neither of us wanted a house cat, so we left her outside, where she was resourceful and a huntress, although she definitely wanted to come in.

Several months after Linda's death, I was feeding Cleo on a bitterly cold winter night. A cold front had moved in from the northwest, and it felt arctic. I was shivering and Cleo was shivering, even with her thick fur coat. I thought, "I can't leave this sweet cat out here. I'll let her in for one night."

She walked through the atrium doors to the breakfast room, looked around, and then gave me an appropriate glance which clearly said, "Well, you finally let me into my house. You can stay, but from now on, I'm in charge!" And she has been ever since. She has proved in spades the adage: "Dogs have owners, cats have staff."

I grew up with dogs, as did Linda and our children and now our grandchildren. Cats were strange to me. Thanks to Cleo, I have received a thorough education in the difference in canine and feline, and I have become inordinately attached to this long-haired creature who lives with me, makes me laugh, and gives me comfort.

Like most cats Cleo is very proud of her achievements as a huntress and loves to display her trophies from rats' heads to bird bodies on the deck and the porch. She does a morning patrol of the acreage around the house and spends time on her favorite lookout towers: the garbage can, the wood box, the water oak, the porch bannister, even the breakfast room table! She rotates around the house, as the watch cat on windowsills in every direction, parting the blinds with her paw for a better view. If an enemy approaches, she will definitely be the first alert!

Long naps are her bread and butter along with leftover cereal milk, ice cream, and Cheetos. After a nap, she races at breakneck speed around the house, landing at last on the entry rug and riding it as it slides across the hardwood floor to the wall. I have seen her crouching at the base of the oak tree by the bird feeder with the sun glistening on her white coat, sure that she is camouflaged while stalking the birds on the feeder.

I can almost hear them saying, "Cat, cat by the oak." She leaps. They fly, and she is hanging by one paw, six feet in the air, with a "Where did they all go?" look on her face.

Once, however, I saw her leap and catch a bird in midair over the birdbath, land on the opposite side, and never even moisten her tail in the process. One day she was moving, leopardlike, toward a hole out of which a gopher was spraying dirt. "She'll never catch that gopher in his tunnel," I thought. Surprise! She stabbed her paw into the hole, caught the gopher, put him in her mouth, and paraded past me on the deck with a "Didn't think I could do it, did you, smarty?" look on her face.

When I am working or writing at my desk and she wants more attention, she simply mounts the computer keyboard, sits on it as she faces me, and waits to be petted and stroked. She then moves to the important papers on the desk, lies on them, and goes to sleep.

Such is life with Cleo. But, at the end of the day, she crawls up on my chest in bed, nuzzles me, licks my nose, and then snuggles up at my feet for the night, waking the next morning ready for a fresh salmon treat and another walk around her estate!

She is, in short, an affectionate snob, a consummate clown, and a valued companion.